Look for gold in
San Francisco!

Shirley Climo

1190

CITY!

SAN FRANCISCO

WITHDRAWN

BY SHIRLEY CLIMO

PHOTOGRAPHS BY GEORGE ANCONA

MACMILLAN PUBLISHING COMPANY   NEW YORK

COLLIER MACMILLAN PUBLISHERS   LONDON

With special thanks to
Molly Wright, children's librarian,
Los Altos Public Library, Santa Clara County, California,
who first saw the need for this series.

—S.C.

For Kendra Marcus
—G.A.

The author wishes to thank Dr. Lester Rowntree, Professor of Geography, San Jose State University, for his assistance in reviewing the factual content of this book.

First Edition   Printed and bound in the United States of America

10 9 8 7 6 5 4 3 2 1

The text of this book is set in 12 point ITC Century Light. The photographs were taken on 35mm Kodachrome film and reproduced from color transparencies.

Library of Congress Cataloging-in-Publication Data: Climo, Shirley. City! San Francisco / by Shirley Climo; photographs by George Ancona. — 1st American ed.   p.   cm.
Summary: Describes San Francisco's history, sights and attractions, and people.
ISBN 0–02–719030–7
1. San Francisco (Calif.)—Description—Juvenile literature. 2. San Francisco (Calif.)—History—Juvenile literature. [1. San Francisco (Calif.)] I. Ancona, George. ill. II. Title.
F869.S34C55 1990 979.4'61—dc20   89-32912 CIP AC

AUTHOR'S NOTE

On October 17, 1989, as this book was going to press, a major earth-quake shook the San Francisco Bay Area. Although it was not as strong as the earthquake of 1906, the temblor affected many communities along the San Andreas Fault, killing people and causing billions of dollars' worth of damage. A fifty-foot section of the San Francisco-Oakland Bay Bridge was destroyed, and the upper deck of a two-tiered freeway in Oakland collapsed, crushing the cars below.

The Bay Area remains vulnerable to nature's most destructive force. But, like the phoenix on the San Francisco flag, it will always rise again from the ashes.

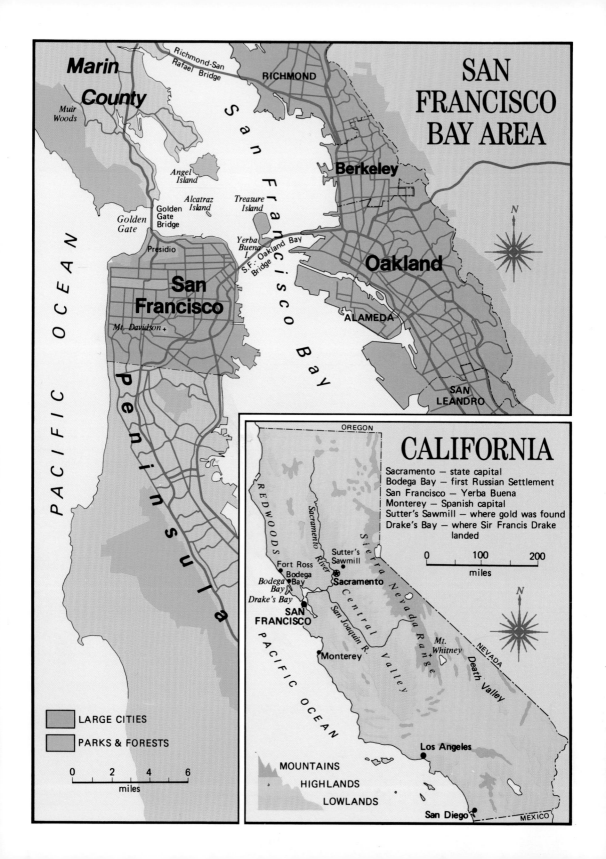

SAN FRANCISCO BAY AREA

Marin County

Muir Woods

Richmond-San Rafael Bridge

RICHMOND

San Francisco Bay

Angel Island

Berkeley

Alcatraz Island

Treasure Island

Golden Gate Bridge

Golden Gate

Yerba Buena I.

Presidio

S.F. Oakland Bay Bridge

Oakland

PACIFIC OCEAN

San Francisco

Mt. Davidson

ALAMEDA

San Francisco Bay

P e n i n s u l a

SAN LEANDRO

N

☐ LARGE CITIES

☐ PARKS & FORESTS

0   2   4   6
miles

CALIFORNIA

OREGON

Sacramento — state capital
Bodega Bay — first Russian Settlement
San Francisco — Yerba Buena
Monterey — Spanish capital
Sutter's Sawmill — where gold was found
Drake's Bay — where Sir Francis Drake
                        landed

0   100   200
miles

R E D W O O D S

Sacramento River

S i e r r a   N e v a d a   R a n g e

Sutter's Sawmill

Fort Ross
Bodega Bay
Bodega Bay
Drake's Bay

Sacramento

SAN FRANCISCO

C e n t r a l   V a l l e y

San Joaquin R.

Mt. Whitney

NEVADA

Death Valley

Monterey

PACIFIC OCEAN

N

Los Angeles

MOUNTAINS

HIGHLANDS

LOWLANDS

San Diego

MEXICO

A.▲ B.▼ C.▼

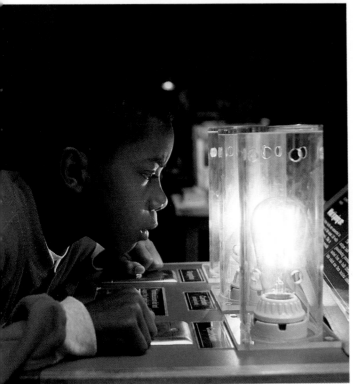

A. The city's hills offer postcard views of San Francisco Bay and Alcatraz Island.
B. At the Exploratorium, a science museum, visitors can touch and tinker with the exhibits.   C. The Bank of Canton stands on Washington Street in Chinatown.

CONTENTS

WELCOME TO SAN FRANCISCO

What's high in the middle, low at the edges, and washed by water on three sides?

San Francisco, of course. If you could see this city from an airplane, you'd guess the answer to the riddle right away.

San Francisco is high in the middle because of its hills. The city is built on forty-three of them. Pale, pastel-colored houses cling to the steep hills like wash spread out to dry.

San Francisco is low at the edges because of its beaches and waterfront. Windswept sand dunes roll up from the sea. Fishing boats and freighters ride at anchor in the bay.

And San Francisco is almost surrounded by salt water. To the west stretches the vast Pacific Ocean. San Francisco Bay lies to the east. Connecting the two is a mile-wide channel known as the Golden Gate.

San Francisco is at the tip of a thumb-shaped piece of land called a *peninsula,* which means "almost an island."

A.◀   B.▲

A. The San Francisco-Oakland Bay Bridge ties the city to Yerba Buena and Treasure Island.   B. San Francisco's tall buildings cluster together at the water's edge.

Smaller cities squeeze up against each other for the entire length of the peninsula. All of these, along with the cities across the bay and other communities across the channel to the north, create a single big picture: the San Francisco Bay Area.

San Francisco isn't just a city by the bay, or on the ocean. It's *in* the water, too. That's because the city includes ten islands. Three of these islands are in San Francisco Bay— Alcatraz Island, Yerba Buena Island, and Treasure Island.

Alcatraz Island is often called "The Rock," for that's exactly what it is. But its name really means "pelican." Spanish sailors named it after that seabird because pelican colonies roosted there. Once a fortress, Alcatraz Island is best known as the site of a famous federal penitentiary. A lighthouse on the island has guided ships since 1854.

Yerba Buena Island is connected to the mainland by the Bay Bridge. Yerba Buena wasn't the first name for this island. Until fifty years ago, it was called Goat Island because of the goats that grazed on its slopes. Its name was changed to honor San Francisco, which was originally called Yerba Buena.

There are no riches buried on Treasure Island. No pirates ever landed here, for this man-made island is much too new. It was constructed in 1939 for a world's fair and is now home to a navy base.

In the Pacific Ocean, about thirty miles offshore, are the Farallon Islands. Their name, in Spanish, means "small pointed islands in the sea." In the last century, San Francisco settlers boated out to these islands to gather the eggs of gulls and murres. As a result, the bird colonies were almost destroyed. In this century, the seven islands have been made wildlife refuges, and most seabirds have returned.

The coastline of California stretches for nearly nine hundred miles. San Francisco lies slightly north of the center of the coast, but its climate is different from that of counties to the north and to the south. The city hardly ever gets as hot as southern California, so you won't find orange trees or date palms growing on the hills. It doesn't get the blustery winters of northern California and Oregon, either. The thermometer seldom falls to freezing in this city, and that's a good thing. Ice and snow would make the hilly streets as slippery as bobsled runs. Still, winter can be cold and damp, for that is the rainy season. If you come to San Francisco between November and April, don't forget your boots and umbrella.

Spring and fall are the sunshine seasons, with a glassy blue bay reflecting a cloudless blue sky. But summertime is fogtime. Although it rarely rains then, in June, July, and August a blanket of fog, thick as wool, often covers the city from night until noon the next day. Fog is San Francisco's natural air-conditioning and keeps the days from getting hot. Usually the temperature is about the same all year, ranging between forty-five and seventy degrees Fahrenheit. A sunny day brings out picnic baskets and sends folks flocking to the beaches, but only fish find the water warm enough for swimming. If you feel shivery, you can always go inland. Within twenty miles, you'll be twenty degrees warmer.

Wind, as well as fog, sweeps in from the ocean, so pack a sweater in your suitcase. One of the city's famous visitors was Mark Twain, the author of *Huckleberry Finn*. He is

A.▲   B.▶

A. Yerba Buena Island lies at the midpoint of the Bay Bridge.
B. *Pacific* means calm, but the waves can be wild at Ocean Beach.

supposed to have said, "The coldest winter I ever spent was a summer in San Francisco."

Whatever the weather, welcome to San Francisco! However you get here—by flying, by driving, or just by thumbing through these pages—stay for a visit. Find out for yourself why San Francisco is a favorite port of call.

T W O

SIX FLAGS FLYING

What if ... the *Mayflower* had sailed to San Francisco?

Long before the Pilgrims landed at Plymouth Rock, even before Jamestown was founded in Virginia, Sir Francis Drake dropped anchor near the site where San Francisco stands today. He planted the English flag, claimed the land for Queen Elizabeth I, and named it Nova Albion, or New Britain. If it were not for what he called the "stynkinge fogges," perhaps Captain Drake would have discovered San Francisco Bay itself. Our country's history might have begun in New Britain instead of in New England.

What if ... San Francisco had become a Russian city?

Two hundred years ago, Russian fur traders hunted seals and otters from the very same Farallon Islands that are now a part of San Francisco. Twenty miles to the north of San Francisco Bay, they built docks and a landing for their ships. The Russians named their settlement Roumianzoff, and claimed the area for *their* queen, Catherine II. But since they were sailors, not settlers, the community did not last.

What if...the Spanish explorers had shrugged their shoulders and forgotten about California?

That almost happened. Spain favored Mexico and treasure-rich South America to what is now our third largest state in area. If not for Father Junípero Serra and the chain of missions that he founded, the story of California, and especially of San Francisco, would be quite different.

In 1542 Juan Rodriguez Cabrillo, a Portuguese navigator exploring for the Spanish king, became the first European to visit Alta, or "Upper," California. The Spaniards named California after a rich and magical island in a book, and their hopes were high that the real place would yield gold for the Spanish crown. First Cabrillo, then two other navigators scouted and charted the California coastline. None found treasure, and none found the entrance to San Francisco Bay. Heavy fog always hid the narrow channel from sight.

Still, San Francisco Bay was not lost to everyone. Costanoan Indians had lived beside it for at least four thousand years. They fished its waters, dug clams from mud flats at low tide, and built their houses from reeds called *tules*, which grew along its shore. Undisturbed and undiscovered, the Indians called the Pacific the "Sunset Sea" and believed that they lived at the edge of the world.

A Spanish soldier, not a sailor, was the first European to see San Francisco Bay. His name was Gaspar de Portolá, and he was not even searching for a harbor. His purpose was to help Father Junípero Serra to establish new missions.

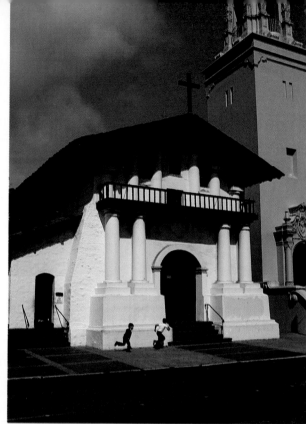

A.▲ B.▶

C.◀ D.▼

A. Near City Hall, statues of a Spanish missionary and a Costanoan Indian honor San Francisco's origins.   B. Mission Dolores is the oldest intact building in San Francisco.   c. Pigeons were early immigrants to San Francisco. The birds were brought to America from Europe more than two hundred years ago.
D. Grave markers in Mission Dolores Cemetery bear dates from gold rush days.

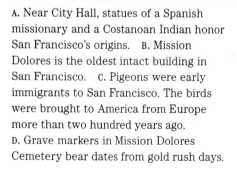

There were already five such settlements supporting Spain's claim to California. Each mission was part church, part fortress, and part farm. In 1769, when Captain Portolá viewed the bay from high on a ridge, he thought he had found a good site for mission number six. What he did not realize was that he was looking down on one of the greatest harbors in the world.

In 1776, a few months after patriots in Philadelphia had signed the Declaration of Independence, Franciscan friars in California dedicated the mission of San Francisco de Asís. Although it was named after Saint Francis of Assisi, the new mission was usually called Dolores, since it stood beside a lake of that name.

The first of the buildings to be completed was a *presidio*, or "fortress," overlooking San Francisco Bay. The Spanish flag waved above its walls, and cannons watched over the harbor below.

Farther inland, the mission itself was built with the help of Indians. Unfortunately the Spanish brought more than religion to the Indians. Old World diseases like measles and smallpox almost completely wiped out the area's Native American population.

Nearly sixty years later, a *pueblo*, or "town," was built in the mud flats by the bay. Wild mint grew there, and a delicious tea, good for shaking off the chills brought on by fog, could be brewed from its leaves. So the town was named after the mint: *Yerba Buena*, or "Good Herb."

Vessels from many countries began visiting Yerba Buena. Cattle ranches had spread out in the nearby valleys, and Yankee schooners came for cowhides from which to make shoes and boots in Boston. Whalers anchored to take on wood and water, and traders sailed around Cape Horn— the tip of South America—to exchange their goods for furs. As more pioneers trekked west, Yankee twangs began to be heard in the muddy alleys of Yerba Buena.

In 1821 Mexico won its independence from Spain and took over Spanish territories north of the Rio Grande. California became a Mexican province, and a fourth flag, the Mexican, flew from flagpoles.

Russian traders did not care who claimed California. They had built their own town just one hundred miles north of San Francisco Bay. With its sturdy stockade, its sixty buildings, and its population of eight hundred persons, Slawianska—later called Fort Ross—was far bigger and stronger than Yerba Buena.

The Russians did not stay long. But Mexico did not relish the United States as a neighbor, either. Earlier, when President Andrew Jackson had asked to buy the San Francisco Bay Area from Mexico for half a million dollars, the reply was no. But what angered the Mexican government most was that their province of Texas broke away and joined the Union as our twenty-eighth state. The whole West was jittery with rumors of war between the United States and Mexico.

An American army captain, John C. Frémont, was determined to keep the Presidio's cannons from firing on any American ships in San Francisco Bay. On a beautiful summer day in 1846, he rounded up a dozen volunteers, borrowed a rowboat, and set out to further disable the Presidio's rusty guns. This meant rowing across the rough and choppy water of the harbor's channel. One of Frémont's men was the famous frontiersman Kit Carson. Holding on tightly to the tossing rowboat, the seasick scout moaned and said, "I'd rather chase grizzly bear in the mountains than ride in this thing!"

The raid was successful, but John Frémont was to remember that afternoon for another reason. He gazed at the waves glistening beneath the sun, and at the orange and yellow poppies crowning the cliffs, and put a lasting label on the channel: the Golden Gate.

Soon John Frémont had hatched a new scheme. Taking a tip from Texas, he and a handful of others proclaimed California an independent state. Although the Republic of California lasted only a few days, it boasted a flag of its own, showing a grizzly bear and a lone star on a field of white. The Bear Republic's was the fifth flag to fly over California.

A month later, the United States and Mexico did go to war. An American naval commander, John B. Montgomery, sailed through the Golden Gate and captured Yerba Buena. The only shot fired was a salute from the guns on Montgomery's ship, the *Portsmouth*. To the tune of "Yankee

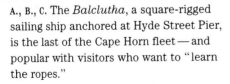

A., B., C. The *Balclutha*, a square-rigged sailing ship anchored at Hyde Street Pier, is the last of the Cape Horn fleet — and popular with visitors who want to "learn the ropes."

OPPOSITE PAGE: A. The flag of the State of California is similar to the banner that flew for the short-lived Bear Republic. B. Today's fresh mint is yesterday's *yerba buena.*   C. John Frémont named this channel the Golden Gate long before a bridge ever spanned it.

A.▲ B.▲ C.▼

Doodle," the Stars and Stripes was raised in Yerba Buena Plaza. That was the sixth flag to fly in the San Francisco Bay Area.

Americans put their stamp on Yerba Buena by renaming the town. Since San Francisco Bay was already on ships' charts, they borrowed that name.

Despite a different flag and a different name, San Francisco was still a sleepy trading post when the Mexican War ended in February 1848. Just days before the peace treaty was signed, though, something happened that would change the city forever. In the foothills of the Sierra Nevada mountains, not far from San Francisco, a man named James Marshall was poking about in the millrace of John Sutter's sawmill. He saw something shiny glinting in the water—*gold!*

THREE

◄──────►

CALIFORNIA
OR BUST!

I shall soon be in San Francisco,
And then I'll look around,
And when I see the gold lumps there,
I'll pick them off the ground!

Treasure hunters sang that song on their way to San Francisco. The city became the gateway to the gold fields, and the setting for the biggest, roughest, toughest parade of people that the world has ever seen. The many thousands of miners who scrambled to dig for gold in 1849 were quickly nicknamed "forty-niners."

Dreamers and drifters came from the world around. In just one year San Francisco's population jumped from eight hundred to thirty thousand! The Golden Gate turned white with the sails of ships. There were whalers and windjammers, barks and sloops, schooners, square-riggers, and even some steamships. Few of the many vessels that sailed in ever sailed out again. Crews deserted and took off for the gold country, too.

A., B. Brass medallions on Lotta's Fountain near the Palace Hotel pay tribute to the forty-niners and to the pioneers. C., D. The stagecoach in the Wells Fargo History Museum brings that time to life.

A.▼   B.▶

C.▼   D.▼

A. When the Chinese prospectors arrived, they brought Chinese cuisine with them. B. A San Franciscan carries a loaf of sourdough bread. C. The original Levi Strauss factory in San Francisco's Mission District still makes the blue jeans that are known around the world.

A. ▲   B. ▲   C. ▼

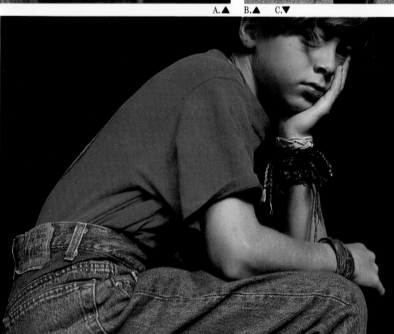

The voyage around Cape Horn was treacherous. Currents swirled and gales blew. But the shortcut across the swamps of Panama, thick with malaria-carrying mosquitoes, was almost as dangerous. Many chose the overland trails in our own country, preferring to face mountain blizzards, searing desert, or hostile Indians. Their covered wagons, called "prairie schooners," were often painted with the slogan CALIFORNIA OR BUST!

When there were enough outposts to supply food and fresh horses, stagecoach service began between Missouri and California. Coaches brought passengers west and carried gold dust and nuggets back east. Both the passengers' pockets and the gold strongboxes were tempting targets for highwaymen.

However the forty-niners got there, the San Francisco they saw was more like a camp than a city. Tents and shanties dotted the hillsides like gopher mounds. Real houses were scarce and few offered a miner more than a place to take off his boots and lay down his head. Most of the "argonauts"—another name given to the gold seekers—were young and single. There were thirty or forty men to every woman in the city, since even married men looking for gold usually left their families behind.

Miners yearned for home cooking. Cooks from many countries opened restaurants, and that is how the San Francisco tradition of "eating in every language" began. Sourdough bread, a forty-niner specialty, became a San Francisco trademark.

There was no one to do the laundry. Dirty shirts were sent all the way to Canton, China, to be washed and ironed— a round-trip of almost a year! News of the gold discovery traveled with them, and soon four thousand Chinese prospectors had come to California. But a washtub still promised a surer fortune than a gold pan, and in 1851 Wah Lee opened the first full-scale laundry in San Francisco.

Every kind of tradesman—from blacksmiths to bankers—hustled to San Francisco. Young Levi Strauss arrived with needles, thread, and bolts of canvas to make tents. When he saw that the pockets of the miners' pants ripped from the weight of gold pouches, he made the heavy canvas into trousers, and fastened brass rivets in the pocket seams to keep them from tearing. These were the first Levi's.

Booming San Francisco was becoming a real city. Twelve daily newspapers were published. Schools and a library opened. There were music halls, theaters, and even an opera house.

But with the good came the bad. As the city grew, so did crime. So many toughs and troublemakers roamed the streets that a new word was coined for them: *hoodlums*. The waterfront was dubbed the "Barbary Coast," after the pirates' lair on the North African shore. People hid behind barred doors in this wild and wicked West. For peace and protection, groups of men formed Vigilance Committees. These Vigilantes policed the streets, but even they were helpless against San Francisco's number one enemy: *fire!*

FOUR

←——→

UPS AND DOWNS

No one, not even the Vigilantes or the volunteer firemen who battled the blazes, could keep San Francisco from burning. Small fires, often started by looters, were fanned by ocean winds, and the cloth and clapboard shacks flared like haystacks. Six times in three years San Francisco burned to the ground. Six times it was raised up again, each time a little better than before.

Yerba Buena Cove was filled in to make a deep-water anchorage. Where reeds once grew, wharves and stores sprang up. Many of the ships deserted in the gold rush became the bones of new buildings—and are still buried beneath the streets today.

In ten years, gold fever had cooled down. Only a fortunate few ever picked gold lumps off the ground. Most miners returned home with empty pockets.

Some prospectors refused to give up. They searched harder, higher, and on both sides of the Sierra Nevada. The few flakes of gold they unearthed were often mixed with a sticky blue-gray clay. In 1859 a hopeful miner had a bit of the clay tested. *Silver!*

A. New high-rise buildings surround the historic Palace Hotel.   B. The Palace, now the Sheraton Palace, has been restored to its former grandeur.   C. A model of a Pony Express rider in the Wells Fargo History Museum recalls the daring men who galloped mail across the wilderness.

A.▲   B.▲   C.▼

Another magic word, and the second rush was on.

Silver is mined differently from gold. While a prospector with a pickax could dig for gold, machinery was needed to tunnel deep inside the mountains for the silver ore. The few men who owned the mines and could afford the necessary machines became millionaires. They were called silver or bonanza kings. The word *bonanza* originally meant "a rich vein of ore," but now we use it in referring to any good fortune.

Silver rebuilt San Francisco. In 1864 alone, more than one thousand new buildings were put up. Besides building his own personal palace, William C. Ralston, a bonanza king, put up the Palace Hotel, the biggest in the world. It covered a full city block, was seven stories high, and had eight hundred rooms!

Thriving San Francisco supplied the West with daily necessities, such as coffee and calico. It supplied education and entertainment, as well, and provided political leadership. Separated from the rest of the country by mountains and desert, San Francisco was the "Queen City of the Pacific."

Communication was San Francisco's greatest challenge. Even by the fastest clipper ship, it took three months to bring mail from New York City to San Francisco. Overland routes were just as slow. Then, in 1860, the Pony Express began. For five dollars, a letter could gallop across the continent in just ten days.

An exhausted Pony Express messenger brought west the news of the firing on Fort Sumter in South Carolina. The Civil War had begun. Although the fighting was far away, the city got ready. San Franciscans feared an attack on their harbor by Confederate ships, or even by British gunboats. Alcatraz Island was heavily armed, and Fort Point, the biggest rock stronghold west of the Mississippi, mounted 127 cannons. Fortunately neither fortress had to fire a shot. Fort Point still stands sentry in the shadows beneath the Golden Gate Bridge.

Five years after the Civil War ended, when the North and the South were reunited, the East and the West were finally connected, as well. Telegraph wires were strung, and in 1869 the last tie was laid and the final spike driven for the transcontinental railroad.

The Central Pacific was the name of the western section of the railroad. Charles Crocker, Collis P. Huntington, Mark Hopkins, and Leland Stanford, nicknamed the "Big Four," were the men who built it. But those who really worked on the railroad "all the livelong day" were the thousands of workers, called *coolies*, brought from China. Coolie comes from the Chinese words *Ku li,* meaning "hard toil." When the railroad was completed, these workers lost their jobs. They moved to San Francisco's "Little China," making it the largest Chinese community outside of Asia. Because Chinese labor was cheaper, San Franciscans feared for their own jobs. In 1882 Congress passed the Chinese Exclusion

A. Messages sent on a telegraph key, like this one in the Wells Fargo History Museum, helped to put the Pony Express out of business.   B. Fort Point was ready to defend San Francisco during the Civil War.

A.▲   B.▼

A.▲ B.▼

A. From the roots of Little China grew the well-established Chinatown of today. B. Shoppers and sightseers crowd a street in Chinatown.

Act, barring Chinese immigration. It was to be the first of many anti-Asian laws.

For the Big Four, riches rolled in with the trains. Their mansions, along with those of the bonanza kings, crowned the heights of San Francisco. Fern Hill had so many of these million-dollar manors that its name was changed to Nob Hill. *Nob* is short for *nabob,* a wealthy person. By mistake, some people spelled the name "Knob" Hill. Others, making no mistake, called it "Snob" Hill.

Getting up and down Nob Hill and other hills was difficult. A Scotsman named Andrew Hallidie solved the problem. He invented a tram car, which, when fastened to a cable in the street, could be pulled up or eased down the steepest grade. In 1873, when Hallidie's tram rolled down Clay Street at a breathtaking nine miles an hour, the cable car was born.

Before the close of the century, another Scotsman had left his mark—a green one—on San Francisco. John McLaren created a blooming oasis from windswept sand dunes. His Golden Gate Park stretched inland from the ocean for four miles, becoming the world's largest man-made park. "Uncle John" McLaren planted almost one million trees and was park superintendent until his death at the age of ninety-six. He, more than anyone else, made San Francisco beautiful.

The gold rush turned San Francisco into an international city. Wave after wave of newcomers from all over the world followed the forty-niners, and by 1870 San Francisco was already the tenth-largest city in the United States. By the close of the century, San Francisco had become a fashionable city, also, with hotels, restaurants, theaters, museums, and the world's biggest opera house. San Francisco had reached the top. Then, on April 18, 1906, it tumbled down.

With a warning rumble, the ground began to shake. It shuddered and rolled for only half a minute, but that was enough to make San Francisco fall as if it were made of kindergarten blocks. Buildings tilted and sagged. Facades and chimneys crashed into the streets. Pavements cracked, stoves overturned, and pipes burst. What had not fallen caught fire, and San Francisco burned for three days. When the wind finally shifted and the fire was controlled, 512 blocks of buildings had been destroyed. Five hundred people were dead or missing, and two hundred fifty thousand others were homeless.

San Francisco became a camp again. People had to cook in the streets. Families lived in tents in Golden Gate Park or in hastily constructed cabins called "earthquake cottages." Then, as it had done before, San Francisco began to rebuild and renew.

A. Visitors can watch the winding gears for San Francisco's cable cars at work in the Cable Car Museum.   B. In preparation for the next run, cable cars are swung around on turntables.
C. When "silver king" James Flood lived in this Nob Hill mansion, the fence was polished every day of the year except Christmas.   D. Here is a gull's-eye view of Golden Gate Park.

A.◀   B.▲   C.▼

D.▼

FIVE

←——————————→

THE CHANGING FACE OF SAN FRANCISCO

San Francisco puts on its best face at sunset. Then violet hills stand out in profile against a ruddy sky.

The tallest of San Francisco's forty-three hills is Mount Davidson. It climbs for over nine hundred feet. Once bald-headed, Mount Davidson is now covered with pine and eucalyptus trees planted by schoolchildren one hundred years ago.

Nearly as high are Mount Sutro and the grassy-knolled Twin Peaks. An Indian legend says that, in the beginning, the Twin Peaks were joined together as husband and wife. The couple argued so long and loudly that the disgusted Sky Spirit threw a lightning bolt and split them in two.

All the hills have names, if not stories. Telegraph Hill earned its name in gold rush days, when a man with sema-phore flags stood on its summit and signaled the arrival of ships. The name Russian Hill is older than the city of San Francisco itself. Two centuries ago, when a Russian sailor died, his ship would put in to San Francisco Bay to bury the seaman on land. So many were buried on top of Russian Hill that the cemetery gave the hill its name. Lombard Street, which wiggles down the hill, is said to be the "crookedest street in the world."

Over the years, San Franciscans have moved or made over their mountains. The heights are crisscrossed with alleys and avenues, clogged with cars and buses. High-rise buildings dominate the skyline and block the peaks from view. Some hills have had tunnels bored through them, and Mount Sutro is topped with a TV transmitting tower that looks as if it had been put together from a giant erector set. Telegraph Hill, once gently rounded, now slides steeply toward the bay. During the gold rush, sailors scooped away the soil near the shoreline to use as ballast for their boats. Winter rains further eroded the hillside. In this century, Rincon Hill lost its head so that the hill could be used as an anchorage for the Bay Bridge.

Many of the changes in San Francisco have been good. The disaster of 1906 forced the city to give itself a face-lift. First to topple in the earthquake were structures built on swampy landfill. First to burn in the fire were rickety and ramshackle wooden buildings. That meant good riddance to much of the wicked Barbary Coast, where rosy-bricked Jackson Square stands today.

All of Little China was lost in the fire. But the Chinese rebuilt their "city within a city" right away. The new Chinatown was even more colorful than the original.

A few buildings withstood both shake and fire. Blazes raged around the Old Mint for seven hours. But workers within did not desert the "Granite Lady" and protected $200 million from looters.

To stop the fire from spreading, whole city blocks had to be dynamited. In clearing the roads of rubble, Market Street was widened to an avenue, becoming the city's most important thoroughfare.

City Hall burned down. A magnificent building replaced it, patterned after the capitol in Washington, D.C.

San Francisco had learned a lesson. So that the city would not collapse again, buildings were constructed on firm foundations. So that San Francisco would not go up in flames once more, engineers drew plans to supply water from the Sierra Nevada mountains.

San Franciscans decided to celebrate the rebuilding of their city and the building of the Panama Canal. In 1915 they invited the world to a party called the Panama-Pacific Exposition. Although war had broken out in Europe, the fair was still a huge success, and nineteen million people poured through the gates.

World War I brought army garrisons, naval forces, and service families to San Francisco. But the war's end left a shortage of houses and jobs, and that meant labor problems. The waterfront, especially, was the scene of many strikes.

Partly to provide jobs, partly to improve transportation, the city began building two enormous bridges. The San

A.▲ B.▼

C.▲ D.▼

A. Coit Tower, located on Telegraph Hill, is 210 feet tall and the favorite lookout for San Franciscans. B. A school bus moves into one of the city's tunnels. C. Lombard Street twists down Russian Hill in nine hairpin turns. D. San Francisco's City Hall looks like the capitol in Washington, D.C., but it's even taller.

A. The Old Mint holds a $5 million treasure in gold bars.   B. Although souvenir coins are as big as silver dollars, they're made of bronze. C. Visitors stamp out coins on an 1869 press at the Old Mint.

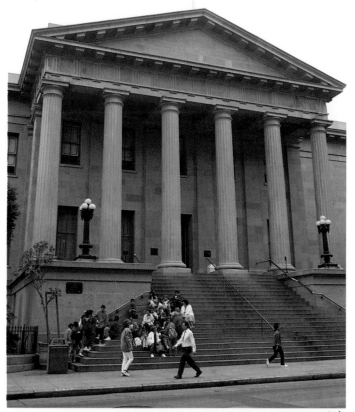

A.▲   B.▲   C.▼

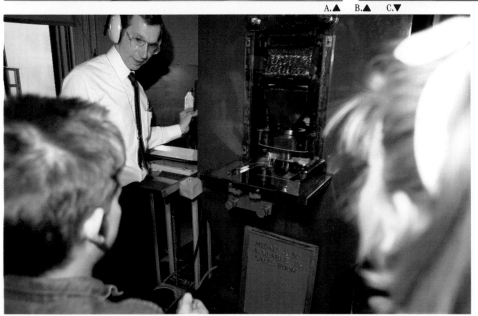

Francisco-Oakland Bay Bridge was completed in November 1936. For the first time, automobiles could drive the eight-and-a-quarter miles across the bay, and the busy ferryboats were no longer needed. Six months later, the Golden Gate Bridge was opened to traffic. Its orange towers and cables, soaring over the mile-wide channel, became a symbol for San Francisco.

The completion of these bridges was reason enough for another world's fair. A magical, man-made fairyland was built in the bay for the fair: Treasure Island. San Francisco opened the Golden Gate International Exposition in 1939. And the people who rushed to it were called . . . thirty-niners! But once again the world was going to war, and when the fair closed, Treasure Island became a naval base.

World War II changed San Francisco almost as much as the gold rush had. During the gold rush, men and supplies sailed in through the Golden Gate. During World War II, a million and a half men and thousands of tons of material sailed out beneath the bridge to the Pacific battlefields. The need for ships was urgent, and so was the need for people to build them. Workers from all around the country swarmed to the shipyards in the San Francisco Bay Area.

As the war neared a close, San Francisco was chosen for an important event. In 1945 representatives from countries all over the world met beneath the gilt dome of San Francisco's opera house to organize the United Nations. The War Memorial Opera House had been built to honor the dead of World War I, and it was there, in 1951, that President Harry S Truman signed the peace treaty that officially ended World War II.

▶   ▶   ▶

There is no typical San Franciscan. Almost every face in the human family is seen here. The speech of almost every nation echoes in the streets, and dishes from almost everywhere in the world are cooked in the kitchens of San Francisco.

Spanish was the language of the settlers of Yerba Buena. That tongue is still heard, but now the words are spoken by Hispanic-Americans from Central and South America.

A handful of black people arrived in San Francisco during the gold rush. But thousands more came to build and launch the ships during World War II.

Congress ended restrictions on Asian immigration in 1965. Now Chinese and Japanese neighborhoods are as San Franciscan as the cable cars. And each year more and more Pacific peoples join them. Today Koreans, Vietnamese, Filipinos, Cambodians, Laotians, Thais, Malaysians, and Samoans are San Franciscans, too.

The Golden Gate Bridge is the city's welcome sign to Asian immigrants. By the close of this century, Asian faces will be in the majority in the San Francisco Bay Area. And San Francisco, Queen City of the Pacific, will be the first predominantly Asian-American city in the United States.

The Golden Gate Bridge, painted
orange to make it visible in any weather,
is one of San Francisco's popular sights.

The ethnic variety of San Franciscans is evident throughout the city.

←——————————————→

EXPLORING SAN FRANCISCO

Gaspar de Portolá was the first explorer to see San Francisco Bay. Today's explorers cannot be the "first," but there is plenty to do and see in and around San Francisco that Captain Portolá never even dreamed of.

IN DOWNTOWN SAN FRANCISCO

▸ Hang on! Ride a cable car.

▸ Visit the Cable Car Museum, and see *how* cable cars stop and start.

▸ Go through the dragon gate to Chinatown, into an exciting confusion of sights and smells and sounds. The jumpiest time to visit is late January or early February, when firecrackers pop for Chinese New Year. But in any season, taste a ginger ice-cream cone, or try some *dim sum—* a variety of Chinese delicacies.

▸ Climb the steep steps up Telegraph Hill to watch the ships in San Francisco Bay. Take the elevator to the top of Coit Tower for an even better view.

▶ Gaze at gold worth millions of dollars at the Old Mint. Stamp out a coin of your own—in bronze.

▶ Stop to touch Ruth Asawa's circular sculpture at Union Square. School children modeled in flour-and-water dough many of the San Francisco scenes for this bronze artwork.

▶ See something old: Mission Dolores, the only building still standing from Spanish days.

▶ See something much newer: *Nihonmachi*—Japantown—with its Peace Pagoda.

AROUND SAN FRANCISCO

▶ See something inspiring. San Francisco has wonderful art museums, including the M. H. deYoung Memorial Museum, the California Palace of the Legion of Honor, and the Museum of Modern Art. Toys from around the world have found homes at the San Francisco International Toy Museum, and three hundred merry-go-round animals now reside at the American Carousel Museum.

BY THE BAY

▶ Walk across the Golden Gate Bridge. Feel the span sway—and look down if you dare!

▶ Walk the ramparts at old Fort Point, which hunches beneath the Golden Gate Bridge. Watch the cannon drills, and join the tours given by rangers in Civil War dress. On dark winter days, special tours are lighted only by candle lanterns.

A.▲ B.▼ C.▲ D.▼

A., B. The Japanese Tea
Garden   C. The Camera
Obscura at the Cliff House
D. The Marina

A. Ruth Asawa's circular sculpture B. The Cannery
C. The San Francisco International Toy Museum
D. At the American Carousel Museum E. Going to Hyde Street Pier F. At the pier

A. ▲　B. ▼　C. ▼　D. ▼

E. ▼　F. ▼

▶ Drive through the Presidio. It is part of the Golden Gate National Recreational Area, a public preserve that takes in many of the scenic areas in and about San Francisco, including several that are mentioned here. The Presidio's grounds are a huge park overlooking the bay. The Presidio Army Museum, housed in an old military hospital, shows relics from Spanish times through the 1906 earthquake and fire.

▶ Look, listen, pull, push, and punch at the Exploratorium. This is a museum where you can explore everything.

▶ Visit the National Maritime Museum at Aquatic Park. You can make history of your own by climbing aboard the square-rigger *Balclutha* or by going down in the *Pampanito*, a World War II submarine.

▶ Don't skip the ships at the National Park Service's Hyde Street Pier. Berthed there are a three-masted schooner, a ferry, a scow, a tug, and a side-wheeler.

▶ Check out Fort Mason's *Jeremiah O'Brien*, a Liberty Ship. Convoys of these lumbering freighters carried supplies across both the Atlantic and Pacific oceans during World War II.

▶ Shop at three old waterfront landmarks, which are now malls. Ghirardelli Square used to be a chocolate factory. Try a hot-fudge sundae. The Cannery was once just that, a fruit-packing center. Pier 39 is lined with shops, not ships, and has a double-decker carousel.

▶ Snack on a shrimp cocktail, or eat crab straight from a steaming outdoor pot on the sidewalk at Fisherman's Wharf, which still harbors the fishing fleet.

ON THE ISLANDS

▶ Take a breezy ride on a boat to Alcatraz Island. A ranger will show you through the federal penitentiary. When a cell door there clangs shut behind you, you'll understand what prisoners mean by being "locked in the slammer."

▶ Bring your bicycle along to Angel Island. Just north of the city limits in the bay, this island was once an immigration station, but now it's an undisturbed nature preserve.

▶ Go by car, not boat, to Treasure Island. Visit the Navy Marine Corps Coast Guard Museum there, and ring the huge fog bell.

IN GOLDEN GATE PARK

▶ Jog, stroll, or roller-skate along the park's twenty-seven miles of paths.

▶ Visit the Buffalo Paddock, where the buffalo roam.

▶ Paddle or pedal a boat on Stow Lake.

▶ Sail a model boat on Spreckels Lake.

▶ Ride a horse. There's a stable, with lessons if you wish.

▶ Ride the old carousel, as children have since 1912, and visit the miniature farm at Children's Playground. It's one of the country's oldest areas built especially for children.

A. The Palace of Fine Arts   B., C., D., E. At the Exploratorium, within the Palace of Fine Arts

OPPOSITE PAGE   A. At the Steinhart Aquarium   B. Ruth Asawa's mermaid fountain at Ghirardelli Square   C., D. At Fisherman's Wharf

A.▼   B.▶

C.▼   D.▼   E. ▼

A.▲   B.▲   C.▼   D.▼

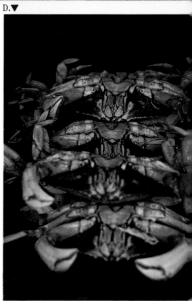

► Look into another world from the moon bridge in the Japanese Tea Garden. The tea garden is almost one hundred years old!

► Wander the huge halls at the California Academy of Sciences. Look and listen to large-as-life exhibits from the world of nature: Wild California, African Safari, and Life through Time, a prehistoric room that's big on dinosaurs!

► See a sky show at the Morrison Planetarium at the Academy.

► Shake in a "safequake," a man-made earthquake, at the planetarium.

► Save lots of time for the Steinhart Aquarium. While you stand still, ocean creatures will circle you in the Fish Round-about. Then go to admire the dolphins, and see penguins being fed. Gaze at alligators and crocodiles, which look as if they'd like to eat you!

AT THE OCEAN

► Watch the waves on the Pacific coast. They may not be any wetter than those on the Atlantic seaboard, yet because of the westerly winds, they're certainly bigger and wilder. A walk along Ocean Beach is an adventure, but if you'd rather see the surf from a safer distance, there are lookouts from the Cliff House. Although the original restaurant burned down, San Franciscans have been coming to this special seaside spot since 1863. On a clear day you can see the Farallon Islands, and on any day you can look at and listen to the sea lions on Seal Rocks.

▶ Go to Fort Funston, an old military reservation, and stare up at daring hang gliders dangling overhead. Walk the wheelchair-accessible Loop Trail there.

▶ Be sure you don't miss San Francisco Zoo. Besides the more common animal compounds and grottoes, there's a Children's Zoo, with a baby animal nursery; the Nocturnal Gallery, where you step from daylight to moonlight to see animals that are awake only at night; the Gorilla World; and the Insect Zoo, first of its kind in California. For an informative four-mile safari through the park, ride the Zebra Zephyr.

▶ Try some do-it-yourself exploring. You're sure to discover other fascinating things to do and see in San Francisco.

SEVEN

A POCKETFUL
OF FACTS

CALIFORNIA

In 1850 California became the thirty-first state admitted to the Union. Admission Day, September 9, is a state holiday.

The capital of California is Sacramento.

California is our most heavily populated state, with about twenty-seven million people. It is the third largest state in area, after Alaska and Texas. Fifty-eight counties stretch from the Oregon border in the north to Mexico in the south.

California's major industry is agriculture.

California's Mount Whitney is the highest point in the "lower" United States. It rises 14,495 feet. Sixty miles away is the lowest point: California's Death Valley, 282 feet below sea level.

California has the world's tallest trees—the California redwood—and the world's oldest—the bristlecone pine. In its mountains are found the largest land birds in North America—the California condors.

A. Muir Woods, a stand of redwoods just north of San Francisco   B. Monument to Science and Industry in the Financial District   C. City Hall, recreated on Ruth Asawa's circular sculpture   D. Flag of the city of San Francisco

A.◀   B.▼

C.▼   D.▼

STATE SYMBOLS

State bird: California quail

State tree: California redwood

State animal: Grizzly bear (now extinct in California)

State fish: Golden trout

State motto: *Eureka!* (Greek for "I found it!")

State colors: Blue and gold

State nickname: The Golden State

State flag: A white field with a red star in the upper left-
hand corner and a grizzly bear on a green patch in the
center. A red band borders the bottom of the flag.

SAN FRANCISCO

San Francisco was founded in 1835 as Yerba Buena. The
American flag flew over it for the first time on July 9, 1846.

San Francisco is both a city and a county. The mainland
area is less than forty-six square miles, making it one of the
smallest cities in the United States.

The population of San Francisco is about seven hundred
fifty thousand, but the whole Bay Area population numbers
close to six million.

San Francisco is governed by a mayor and a Board of
Supervisors, each elected for four-year terms.

The tallest point in the city is Mount Davidson, at 938
feet, and the lowest is at sea level.

The major industries in the San Francisco Bay Area
include electronics and biotechnology. San Francisco itself

is a financial center, but its biggest industry is tourism. That's *you!*

CITY SYMBOLS

San Francisco motto: *Gold in peace, iron in war*

San Francisco colors: Gold and black

San Francisco flag: White, with a legendary bird called a phoenix rising from a ring of fire

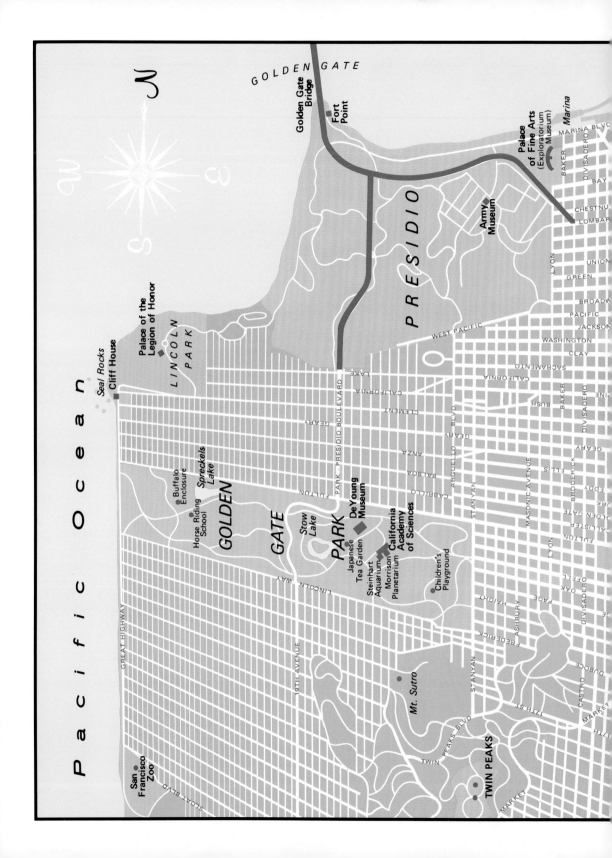

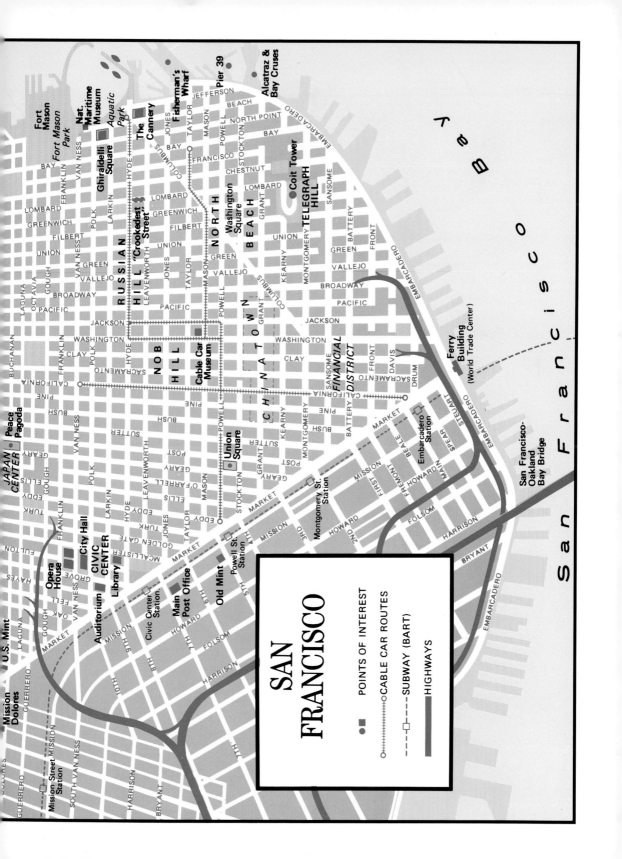

SAN FRANCISCO

- ■● POINTS OF INTEREST
- ○○○○○ CABLE CAR ROUTES
- ----□---- SUBWAY (BART)
- ▬ HIGHWAYS

I N D E X